COUNTRIES OF THE WORLD

England

Gareth Stevens Publishing

MILWAUKEE

Maree Lister, an Australian, has taught in the British Council for many years and has worked on a range of educational materials. She has also lived and worked in England and frequently returns there for visits. Marti Sevier, an American, also teaches at the British Council and has many years' experience in producing teaching materials and working with the British.

Written by
MAREE LISTER AND MARTI SEVIER

Edited by
JONATHAN GRIFFITHS

Designed by
LYNN CHIN NYUK LING

Picture research by
SUSAN JANE MANUEL

First published in North America in 1998 by
Gareth Stevens Publishing
1555 North RiverCenter Drive, Suite 201
Milwaukee, Wisconsin 53212 USA

For a free color catalog describing
Gareth Stevens' list of high-quality books
and multimedia programs, call
1-800-542-2595 (USA)
1-800-461-9120 (CANADA)
Gareth Stevens Publishing's
Fax: (414) 225-0377
See our catalog, on the World Wide Web:
http://gsinc.com

© **TIMES EDITIONS PTE LTD 1998**
Originated and designed by
Times Books International
an imprint of Times Editions Pte Ltd
Times Centre, 1 New Industrial Road
Singapore 536196
http://www.timesone.com.sg/te

Library of Congress Cataloging-in-Publication Data
Lister, Maree.
England / by Maree Lister and Marti Sevier.
p. cm. — (Countries of the world)
Includes bibliographical references and index.
Summary: Introduces the geography, history, economy, government, culture, food, and people of England.
ISBN 0-8368-2125-4 (lib. bdg.)
1. England—Juvenile literature. [1. England.] I. Sevier, Marti. II. Title.
III. Series: Countries of the world (Milwaukee, Wis.)
DA27.5.L57   1998
942—dc21   98-13067

Printed in Singapore

1 2 3 4 5 6 7 8 9 02 01 00 99 98

Contents

AN OVERVIEW OF ENGLAND

England has had its share of heroes and villains, and has recorded great successes and terrible failures. A separate country in its own right, it is also the center of the nation known as Great Britain, made up of England, Scotland, and Wales. Northern Ireland combines with Great Britain to form the United Kingdom. England has a long and influential history and has played a significant role in many of the events that have shaped the modern world. The form of government known as parliamentary democracy has its origins in England. Few other nations can match its hundreds of years of achievements in government, economy, arts, science, exploration, sports, and war.

Opposite: **Feeding pigeons in Trafalgar Square, London.**

Below: **A quiet fishing village — an ideal setting for artists.**

THE FLAG OF ENGLAND

A red cross on a white field, the English flag is the cross of St. George, the patron saint of England. The flag of the United Kingdom, the Union Jack, is a combination of the cross of St. George, the cross of St. Andrew, and St. Patrick's Cross, which together represent England, Scotland, and Ireland. Shrouded in myth and legend, St. George probably lived in the third century. The most famous story concerning George tells of his slaying a dragon while rescuing a maiden. He is revered as a Christian martyr and was raised to sainthood in the fourteenth century.

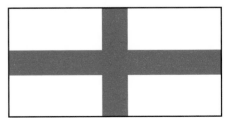

Geography

England encompasses 50,000 square miles (129,500 square kilometers) and makes up just over half of the total area of the United Kingdom. To the north is Scotland, and to the west, Wales. The country is only 360 miles (580 km) from north to south and 330 miles (531 km) from east to the westernmost point, Land's End, in Cornwall.

The Landscape

A relatively low country, with its highest peak, Scafell Pike, only 3,210 feet (978 meters) high, England lacks the dramatic contrasts of North America's Rocky Mountains or any lakes as big as one of the Great Lakes in the United States. Scafell Pike is found in the Lake District, in the northwest. This area was carved by glacial action during the ice age, and its mountains and many lakes, notably England's largest, Lake Windermere, make it the most visited area of England. East of the Lake District and running south to the Peak District in central England, is a mountain range

Below: **A farmhouse in the Cumbria region in northwest England. England is not a mountainous country, but the Cumbrian Mountains include the country's highest peak, Scafell Pike. The southwestern area of England is also hilly and mountainous, with peaks over 2,000 feet (609 m) near Dartmoor. To the south, the famous white cliffs of Dover face the English Channel and France.**

called the Pennine Chain. England's longest river is not very long, but it is one of the most famous rivers in the world. The Thames (TEMZ), a tidal river, begins at Seven Springs in the Cotswold Hills and winds slowly through hills and valleys to London, a length of 210 miles (338 km).

Wetlands

A special feature of the English landscape is its wetlands. These low-lying, swampy areas give valuable refuge to bird life and plants. Peat bogs are formed when mires fill in with plants such as water lilies and reeds. These plants gradually collapse into a thick layer. As more plant layers grow, they eventually lose contact with the water in the mires and must depend on rainfall for moisture. This causes the plant-layers underneath to become acidic, making it impossible for trees to grow. What grows instead is moss, and so bogs are formed. The peat formed in the bog is a traditional fuel source, still used in some parts of Britain. Archaeologists have unearthed ancient human remains remarkably preserved in the acidic environment.

Above: **Lobster pots on the quayside at Mevagissey in Cornwall. Located in the westerly wind belt, England's coastal areas are also exposed to strong winds, or gales, with the southwest suffering the most: Cornwall has strong gales on over thirty days a year, on average.**

Seasons

Although most English people complain about the weather, the country's climate, although changeable, is generally mild. Snow, especially in the north, does not last for long, and rarely do people experience blizzards. Although winters can be cold, temperatures rarely go below freezing due to the effects of ocean currents. Nor do temperatures rise much higher than 68° Fahrenheit (20° Centigrade) in the summer.

Rain falls year round, giving England its reputation for dreary weather. Strong winds, called gales, are quite common in the winter months. They have combined with stormy seas over millions of years to form much of England's spectacular and rugged coastline. The hours of daylight vary significantly between summer and winter due to the country's geographical latitude, which is above 50° north.

THE LAKE DISTRICT

The traditional image of the Englishman with his umbrella exists for good reason! The wettest part of the country is the Lake District, with an annual average of about 80 inches (203 centimeters) of rainfall. Styhead Tarn, in the same region, claims the record amount of rainfall — over 170 inches (432 cm) a year!
(A Closer Look, page 50)

Left: Fields of daffodils are a common sight in England. The bulbs of these flowers were once used in medicines. About twenty-two thousand plant species grow in Britain. The northern moors, for example, are covered with heather, cotton grass, and other grasses, while the common poppy is often found in cornfields in the south. Foxglove, which prefers acidic soil, often grows in meadows, while the common rock-rose grows best in dry, sunny areas in calcium-rich soils containing chalk or limestone.

Plants and Animals

The deciduous forests of oak, ash, beech, and elm that once covered England have mostly been cleared for farming, a process that began in the Middle Ages. Today only about 7 percent of the land is forested.

The North Sea was one of the world's richest fishing grounds, and the catch still provides an important part of the English diet. England has twenty-three indigenous species of freshwater fish: all can be found in lakes and streams in Yorkshire, and most in Norfolk. In the early 1900s, North American freshwater fish such as pumpkinseed, brook trout, and largemouth bass were introduced, mainly to water bodies on large estates.

Birdwatching in England is an obsession with many, and each region has its special feathered residents and visitors. From the chirpy robin to the once abundant but now carefully protected red kite, there are about one hundred and thirty-five kinds of birds that live in England all year and another fifty-five that pass through when migrating. The red deer, England's largest wild animal, and the roe deer are the only native English deer. Foxes, badgers, stoats, and voles are commonly seen in country and village areas. Atlantic gray seals live along the coasts of Scotland, the west of England, and Ireland. The common seal lives in shallower water along the east coast of England, as well as in Scotland and Ireland. England has just a few species of snakes — only the adder, shy but with a venomous bite, threatens the careless.

Top: **A red fox cub at home in a wooded area of the English countryside. The fox is considered a pest by farmers, but many people believe it should be protected.**

Above: **The rose is the floral emblem of England.**

LOVE FOR ANIMALS

The English are known for their love of animals, and many homes have at least one pet.
(*A Closer Look, page 52*)

History

England's history spans many thousands of years. Here is a general picture of important times, people, and events.

The Romans

Julius Caesar invaded England in 55 B.C., defeating the Celts and beginning a turbulent Roman rule that lasted until around A.D. 406, when all Roman troops were recalled to Rome. The local tribes resisted the Romans but were no match for their weapons and army. In A.D. 61, one famous rebel, Queen Boudicca, led a revolt against the Romans, but they retaliated with an army of ten thousand and crushed the rebels.

The Rise of Christianity

Christianity reached England in Roman times. During the Dark Ages that followed, pagan gods were again worshiped in England, although Christianity flourished in Europe and especially in Scotland. In A.D. 597, Christianity was reestablished, and in 663 the pope was recognized as the supreme authority in England.

STONEHENGE

Arrangements of huge stones were built in England by early settlers. Their purpose remains a mystery, but some, like Stonehenge, are still standing today.

(A Closer Look, page 64)

Below: **Although no longer in use, this Roman bathhouse is a reminder of the fact that England was once part of the Roman Empire.**

The Middle Ages

This period, also known as the Medieval era, covers almost three hundred years. The beginning was dominated by the Crusades, which began around 1100. European Christians went to the Holy Land to free it from the Turkish Muslims. England's King Richard I, known as Richard the Lionheart, spent many years fighting in the holy wars.

When Richard died fighting, his unpopular brother John became king. In 1214, the English barons revolted and forced the king to sign the Magna Carta, the "Great Charter," which guaranteed certain rights — people could not be punished without a trial, and taxes could only be raised with the barons' agreement. This was the beginning of the English parliamentary system. In the thirteenth and fourteenth centuries, parliament was strengthened. By the reign of Edward III (1327–1377), it had a regular meeting place, Westminster, where parliament has met ever since.

THE DARK AGES

The period of one hundred and fifty years after the Romans' departure is known as the Dark Ages because few records survived the fighting and destruction. The people called Britons had to defend themselves against the Picts, the Welsh, the Saxons from Germany, and Irish pirates. The Britons fought back with the help of some paid Saxons who stayed. These new settlers, called Angles, Saxons, and Jutes, banded together against the Britons. By A.D. 600, the Anglo-Saxons, as they are often referred to, were masters of the lowlands, and the country was called England, the land of the Angles.

The Reformation

In 1534, after a dispute with the Catholic Church, Henry VIII set up a new Protestant Church, with the king as its supreme head instead of the pope. This was the beginning of what is now the Church of England, or Anglican Church. Henry's changes came during a period of time known as the Reformation, a religious revolution within Christianity that led to the formation of Protestant religions throughout Europe. The following years in England saw an ongoing struggle between Catholic and Protestant monarchs. Eventually, under Elizabeth I (1558–1603), the Church of England became the dominant religion, but people were allowed to follow the religion they pleased, as long as they did not threaten Elizabeth's rule.

Above: **The Duke of Wellington won lasting fame for his defeat of Napoleon's French forces at the Battle of Waterloo.**

The Empire

By the 1750s, Britain was fighting France in the Seven Years' War, and its colonies, while supplying wealth, were challenging British rule. Under Prime Minister William Pitt, Britain defeated France, weakening French influence in world trade. By 1763, Britain's empire included much of the Americas, Africa, the West Indies, and India, and was a world trade and military power.

But the American colonies wanted to determine their own future, and after a protest in Boston about British taxes, they declared their independence. After seven years of fighting, the British forces surrendered in 1781. American independence was granted in 1783.

At the end of the century, France and Britain were at war again. The French navy was defeated in 1805 by forces led by Lord Nelson at the Battle of Trafalgar. The French army was finally defeated in 1815 at the Battle of Waterloo by forces led by the Duke of Wellington.

Opposite: **Queen Elizabeth I. King Henry VIII began England's move away from the influence of the Catholic Church, a position that was later supported by Queen Elizabeth. This period of changing religious allegiances was known as the Reformation.**

Unionism and the Welfare State

In 1908, old age pensions were introduced for people over the age of sixty-five. The National Insurance Act of 1911 provided people with money, known as the dole, when they became unemployed. But to pay for these welfare reforms taxes were raised, and many discontented workers went on strike. Organized labor in the form of unions wielded great power politically and until recently, unions were closely allied with the British Labour Party.

ROBIN HOOD

Many mythical figures have their origins in English history, including Robin Hood. He fought against the rule of Prince John by robbing from the rich to give to the poor.

(A Closer Look, page 58)

13

Left: In 1900, there were nearly forty million people in Britain. Life expectancy was rising because of improved medicine and living conditions. However, the terrible trench warfare and poison gas attacks of World War I killed many young Englishmen. Women worked in factories and on farms during the war and soon after gained the vote. After the war, Britain was burdened by debt due to war expenses.

The Twentieth Century

When World War II broke out in 1939, Britain was not well prepared. Prime Minister Chamberlain tried to make peace with Hitler, but failed. The new prime minister, Winston Churchill, rallied the people, and the British fought bravely, abroad and at home. During the Battle of Britain, English pilots fought off attacks by the German airforce and prevented a German invasion.

After World War II, Britain was again in serious debt. The shrinking Empire was further weakened when India, Ceylon (Sri Lanka), and Burma became independent in 1947 and 1948. But agriculture, stimulated by war demand, had become more productive and profitable. Advances were made in housing and education, and in 1948, the National Health Service (NHS), which provided free or cheap medical treatment, was created.

In 1973, Britain joined the European Economic Community (EEC). The EEC evolved into the European Union (EU), and the United Kingdom, led by England, plays an important role in shaping its policies and directions.

"THE TROUBLES"

Religious differences between Catholics and Protestants still exist today in Northern Ireland. Protestant Loyalists want to remain a part of Britain, but the Catholic Republicans are opposed to British rule in Northern Ireland.
(A Closer Look, page 70)

SUFFRAGETTES

Fighting for the rights of women, particularly the right to vote, the suffragette movement had a significant impact on English society in the first half of the twentieth century.
(A Closer Look, page 66)

King Henry VIII

King Henry VIII (1491–1547) was the king of England from 1509 to 1547 and is most famous for his many wives and for forming the Anglican Church. In Henry's time, politics and religion were closely allied. In order to continue his family's rule, he needed an heir, preferably a son, to take the throne when he died. His marriage to Catherine of Aragon, his brother's widow, produced a daughter (the future queen, Mary I), but still he wanted a male heir. Henry wanted to end his marriage and marry Ann Boleyn, a lady of the Court, but was forbidden from doing this by the pope. The king's solution was to form a new Church, one that would allow him to divorce. By the time of his death, he had been married six times but only his third wife, Jane Seymour, bore him a son. She herself died in childbirth.

Henry VIII

William Shakespeare

William Shakespeare (1564–1616) is considered the greatest writer in the English language. He wrote mainly for the stage, and his work is still performed throughout the world. He produced many plays including histories, comedies, and romances, but it was the tragedies, such as *Macbeth*, *King Lear*, and *Hamlet* that mark the peak of his skills as a writer and provide one of the highest points in the development of Western literature. In England and most other English-speaking countries, the work of Shakespeare is read and enjoyed by high school and college students alike, although as Hamlet, one of Shakespeare's famous characters, once remarked, this is often a "custom more honored in the breach than the observance."

William Shakespeare

Margaret Thatcher

The Conservative government of Margaret Thatcher (1925–), the first woman prime minister of Britain, was elected into office in 1979. During this time, the Conservatives managed to keep inflation down but did little to reduce unemployment. Margaret Thatcher led the country as head of the Conservative Party for three consecutive terms until 1990. She is considered one of Britain's strongest postwar leaders and is known for her strong views and forceful manner, which earned her the nickname "Iron Lady." She also led the country during the brief but decisive war against Argentina in 1982 over the disputed ownership of the Falkland Islands.

Margaret Thatcher

Government and the Economy

The Role of the Crown

The monarch plays a largely symbolic role in government as commander-in-chief of the armed forces and head of the Church of England and the Commonwealth (a group of nations formerly part of the British Empire). Although called the supreme head of the three branches of government — the legislative, judicial, and executive — the Crown cannot in fact make decisions without the advice of ministers and other leaders, which are part of a group called the Privy Council.

The Government

England is run at the national level by parliament, its legislative, or law-making body. Parliament also provides a forum for debating issues of national importance and provides money for different purposes, such as foreign aid or education. Parliament has two houses, the House of Lords and the House of Commons.

Below: **The Trooping of the Colour, part of the annual Queen's Birthday Parade.**

Above: **The Houses of Parliament, with the famous Big Ben clock tower, in Westminster, London.**

The head of the House of Lords is called the lord chancellor. The House of Commons has 650 members, called members of parliament, or MPs, elected from different areas of the country called constituencies. In Britain, people can vote at age eighteen.

In the British parliament, a proposed law, called a bill, can be introduced either by the government or by an individual MP. It is discussed and, if passed in one house, is then sent to the other. If a bill is passed by both houses, it becomes law. Britain has no written constitution.

The head of the government is the prime minister. The two dominant parties are the Conservative Unionist Party and the New Labour Party.

On a local level, councillors are elected and take responsibility for water, utilities (electricity and gas), garbage collection, police and fire services, and in some areas, health care. Income for both local and national government is derived from taxes. A value added tax (VAT) on consumer items provides additional revenue for the government.

PROTECTING NATURE

The government provides funds to aid environmental groups and preserve natural resources.
(*A Closer Look, page 56*)

The Economy

The United Kingdom ranks as the sixth richest country in the world in terms of per capita income. Since World War II, the economy has moved away from being product-based to being service-based. England has few natural resources, with coal and oil being the most important.

Industry and Trade

England was once a leader in iron and steel production but there have been recent declines in these industries. The British aerospace industry is the largest in western Europe, producing aircraft for both military and civilian purposes. Woolen textiles, carpets, and clothing are still made in the Yorkshire area, where high-quality goods are produced at a relatively low cost. Manufactured goods make up nearly 20 percent of all British exports. The United States and Germany are Britain's biggest trading partners: Germany imports 12.7 percent of all British exports, while the U.S. imports 12.5 percent. Primarily a service industry, tourism is another important source of income.

Above: **North Sea oil, drilled since the 1960s, has resulted in Britain being completely self-sufficient in oil and needing to import only 25 percent of its natural gas. Petroleum products make up 5 percent of all British exports.**

FOSSIL FUELS vs NUCLEAR POWER

Although England has large coal reserves, it also uses nuclear reactors to provide some of its electricity. Many people question the safety of nuclear power and protest its use.
(A Closer Look, page 49)

Agriculture

English farms have undergone major changes in the last fifty years and currently supply about two-thirds of the country's needs. One result of mechanization and increased efficiency is that fewer people are needed to work on farms. Barley and wheat are the most common grain crops. Potatoes, sugar beets, hops for beer, and rapeseed for vegetable oil are also grown.

Transportation

Although England is very small, the country has all major forms of transportation: roads, railroads, airways, and a minor one — canals.

As highways grow in importance, railroads are used much less than they once were. Most freight is now carried by trucks, and most people use private cars to go from place to place.

Britain's major airline is British Airways, one of the first to use the supersonic Concorde aircraft, which flies between London and New York and Washington, D.C. London's Heathrow Airport is the busiest airport in the world for international flights. There is very little internal air traffic in England, because of its small size.

CANALS

Canals had a brief era of glory, only to be replaced by the railroad. They are still used in some parts of the country as a cheap alternative to road transportation as well as for tourism.
(*A Closer Look, page 46*)

Below: **Dairy farming exists in areas of heavy rainfall, where there is rich pasture land. British beef production took a major blow with the destruction of thousands of cows due to "mad cow disease" in 1996.**

People and Lifestyle

England has a highly structured society, characterized by a class system that separates one group from another. The largest of these groups is the middle class, and a middle class lifestyle is the one most English people enjoy. This separation of people according to class is not a formal or legal distinction but the result of customs and cultures formulated over many generations. The existence of a royal family helps to maintain this culture of class in that they

Left: **One visible reminder of the former extent of the British Empire remains in the population of England today. Immigrants, mainly from Commonwealth countries like the West Indies, continue to settle in England, making it a multicultural society. Membership in the European Union also allows for easy movement between countries by its members.**

receive benefits and privileges as a birthright, rather than as a result of their achievements or contributions to society.

In the past hundred years, England has had to adjust to its changing role in world affairs, from a dominant world power controlling a large empire, to a smaller, yet still influential part of the European Union. In general though, English people still enjoy a high standard of living, dividing their time between work and leisure.

Above: **The punk movement began in England and is still popular among some young people in the country. Freedom of expression is an important part of English society.**

Immigration

Before the 1950s, most of England's immigrants came from Europe and especially from Ireland. These days, the largest ethnic minority group in England is people from India, followed by people from the West Indies, and then Pakistan. Other groups include Chinese, Africans, Bangladeshis, and Arabs. Ethnic minorities form around 4 percent of the total population, and over one hundred languages are spoken in Britain.

Left: A traditional view of English life is of an extended family with their own home meeting in the garden for a tea party. This traditional family unit, the nuclear family, is still a strong part of the English identity, particularly among the more conservative sections of society. Families these days tend to be smaller, with usually two or three children.

Family Life

These days, many people choose to have children, but they may also decide not to follow the traditional path of marriage. The nuclear family unit is no longer the norm for many people, and there are as many as two million children being brought up in one-parent families. It is estimated that 30 percent of all children born in England today are born to parents who are not married, but many of these parents live together. Divorce is also more common than it once was.

Whether they are part of a nuclear family or a one-parent family, more women who have children do not stay at home to take care of the children. Some women have to work because of economic necessity, and others work because they enjoy their chosen career. For example, Cherie Blair, the wife of the present prime minister, Tony Blair, is a successful lawyer.

When they are not at work or at school, families in England enjoy many leisure activities. Sometimes they stay home, watching television, doing jobs around the house, playing games, and generally relaxing. At other times, they may go shopping, go to a movie or restaurant, play a sport, or visit other members of their family, such as grandparents, aunts, and uncles.

Education

England has one of the highest literacy rates in the world, with 99 percent of its people able to read and write. English children are required to attend school between the ages of five and sixteen. Only about 24 percent of children go on to university or some other form of higher education.

England follows what is called the National Curriculum, which means that all state school students must study the same subjects, no matter where they live. These subjects are English, mathematics, science, design and technology, information technology, history, geography, music, art, physical education

Below: **Economic hardship forces some homeless people to live on the streets. England's welfare system tries to prevent the problem from becoming widespread.**

(PE), and a modern foreign language, usually French. Most students wear uniforms to school.

Students take many examinations as part of their education. National tests are given at the ages of seven, eleven, and fourteen. These help the school make decisions about the kinds of courses students should take. Sometimes very bright students are given "enrichment" classes that help to challenge their special abilities.

At the age of sixteen, students take "O" levels, which are public examinations given nationwide and graded by a group of educators outside the school. Students must decide fairly early what subjects they will specialize in for this examination. About 75 percent of English students leave school after "O" levels. They may go straight to work or prepare for a job by going to vocational school. Others go on to "A" level examinations in preparation for study at a university or college.

A small percentage of students (6 percent) in the United Kingdom attend private schools, and of these, boarding schools are still popular among some groups of people. Strangely, these schools are referred to as "public schools" in England.

OXFORD AND CAMBRIDGE UNIVERSITIES

Relatively few students go to universities, and only the best enter Oxbridge—Oxford or Cambridge, England's most prestigious universities.

(*A Closer Look, page 54*)

Below: Pre-school and some help from older brothers and sisters prepares children for their school years.

All Work and No Play

Although students are expected to study hard, the English school system also places great emphasis on extra-curricular activities. These include music, Scouts, Brownies, and Guides (the British equivalent of Girl Scouts), hiking, arts and crafts, and a wide variety of sports. English students enjoy cricket, a game somewhat like baseball, and rugby, a rougher game, much like football. Soccer, track and field, gymnastics, swimming, netball, and field hockey are also popular.

Trips and excursions are another important part of school life. In the lower grades, children take trips to places of natural, historical, or cultural importance. Because of the Channel Tunnel (Chunnel), trips to the European continent are now quick and relatively inexpensive, so one popular destination for students is France, where they are expected to put their language skills to use!

Above: **University graduation day is a proud day for students and their families.**

25

Religion

Most English people belong to the Church of England (the Anglican or Episcopal Church) or another Christian denomination. A profile of religion in Britain shows that 47 percent are Anglican, 9 percent are Roman Catholic, 4 percent are Presbyterian, 3 percent are Muslim, 1 percent are Methodist, while 36 percent belong to other religions or do not belong to any religion.

Religious Knowledge is studied as part of the school curriculum in state and independent schools. Religious tolerance and the right to worship as one chooses are legally protected.

Below: **St. Paul's Cathedral was built between 1675 and 1710. Its dome is second in size only to St. Peter's Basilica in Rome.**

Folk Traditions: Goblins, Ghosts, and Enchanted Lakes

Some beliefs of pre-Christian religions still survive as superstitions. They are not generally taken seriously, but many people still enjoy telling the old stories of supernatural happenings. Many of these stories have their origins in the Celtic myths told thousands of years ago.

Hobgoblins or hobs, were considered house spirits — elves or sprites who would clean up the mess left in a house overnight, but also mess up anything left neat! The Cauld ("cold") Lad of Hylton in Sunderland could, so tradition has it, be heard singing "Woe is me!" every night as he went about his business of upsetting things. The best way to get rid of a hob was to give him clothes to wear, then the Cauld Lad, no longer cold, would vanish without a trace.

Land's End in Cornwall is the westernmost part of England, and between it and the Isles of Scilly is said to be a drowned city called Lyonesse. People claim to be able to see the tops of houses

beneath the waves and recall how only one man, Trevalyan, escaped from the rising waters. Some researchers believe Lyonesse may be the lost city of Atlantis. Other tales of drowned cities are told to illustrate how sin is punished; in Wales, a poor man robbed and killed an innocent traveler so he could marry the woman he loved. In their old age, on their wedding anniversary, the island on which they feasted sank into the sea.

Above: **Christmas is a traditional Christian celebration and a time for families to get together for a feast.**

Language and Literature

The History of English

The English language as we know it today came from many people and many places. The original Celtic languages spoken in ancient Britain were gradually pushed out by the language of the Angles and Saxons, who spoke Germanic dialects. Their language became Old English, or Anglo-Saxon.

Left: Geoffrey Chaucer (*c.* 1342/43–1400), writer of *The Canterbury Tales,* was influential in the development of modern English.

28

English Literature

English literature is usually thought to have begun in the seventh or eighth century with the story of the "battle-brave" Beowulf, an Old English story about a Norse hero who slaughtered a fierce monster called Grendel and went on to other feats of bravery. Beowulf, like other early stories, was passed on by word of mouth, since few people could write, and printing presses had not yet been invented.

The Brontë sisters, like Jane Austen before them, were among the first nineteenth-century women writers. Their writing was passionate and powerful. Charlotte Brontë's *Jane Eyre* and Emily Brontë's *Wuthering Heights* are still enjoyed by readers today.

Pirates in the South Seas, Indian jungles, and lost lands inhabited by dinosaurs were the basis for tales of strange adventure by the Victorian writers, Robert Louis Stevenson, Rudyard Kipling, and Arthur Conan Doyle. England offers many literary prizes to writers, and London remains one of the world's largest publishing centers.

England's tradition of appointing poets laureate, who are considered the official poets of the royal court, began in the seventeenth century and continues to this day. Ted Hughes, who was married to the American poet Sylvia Plath, holds the position today and writes both for children and adults. Philip Larkin and Geoffrey Hill are other highly acclaimed English poets.

Below: **In the Victorian era (*c.* 1840–1900), English literature was used as a means of social protest. Charles Dickens (below), who had as a child spent time in the appalling conditions of the workhouses, used his colorful characters and humor, as in *Oliver Twist*, to make social comments about the treatment of the poor.**

29

Arts

Early Art

The farmers of the later Stone Age and the Bronze Age were also artists and architects. Their pottery, especially that of the Beaker Folk, a Bronze Age group, was functional yet decorative. Many of their simple tombs were decorated with stone carvings.

Celtic artists worked for the elite who loved clothes and jewelry. Metal and precious stones were turned into brooches, hand-mirrors, and drinking cups. Celtic warrior lords possessed

SIR FRANCIS DRAKE: PIRATE OR DRAGON?

Before photography, artists were in great demand to produce portraits. Many of these paintings were commissioned by the royal court to commemorate the deeds of famous people. Sir Francis Drake, a favorite of Queen Elizabeth I, was the subject of many paintings after his voyage around the world and his defeat of the Spanish armada. (*A Closer Look, page 60*)

Left: A stained glass window in Canterbury Cathedral. Early artistic expression was often religious in nature, and churches and cathedrals hold many examples of the work of English artists and craftsmen.

helmets, shields, and sword scabbards made of bronze decorated with circles and curves of enamels and gems.

The Romans were great builders, although few of their buildings remain today because wood was used in a lot of the construction. At Bath, Roman engineers harnessed the hot springs and constructed bathhouses. Roman houses often had intricate mosaic floors.

The Anglo-Saxon period was one of the greatest and most innovative periods in English arts. A variety of art forms flourished, ranging from metalwork, stone sculpture, and carvings in ivory, bone, and wood, to manuscripts and embroidered textiles.

A famous tapestry, The Bayeux Tapestry, was produced shortly after 1066, the year of the Norman Conquest. Elaborately embroidered with colored wool, it illustrates the events leading up to and including the Norman Conquest. Originally thought to be the work of Norman embroiderers, many art historians now feel it resembles Anglo-Saxon embroidery traditions.

Above: The West End is a London theater district known around the world for the quality of its productions. English theater has a long history and flourished under the reign of Queen Elizabeth I and the pen of William Shakespeare.

Modern Art and Architecture

In the nineteenth century, the Romantic movement in both literature and the arts began. It questioned many old ideas. Art and literature were being thought about and interpreted for the first time, not just simply looked at or read.

This period produced two great, but different, painters — John Constable and Joseph Turner. Constable painted rural scenes from his native Suffolk but only achieved fame after he died. Turner grew up illiterate in London but managed to gain a place in a Royal Academy art school. He painted historical and mythological subjects, but his landscapes, especially his seascapes, made him famous.

New engineering methods and materials of the Industrial Revolution affected the design of buildings and other objects. Artists and architects began to work more in iron and steel. The

Below: **The work of English sculptor Henry Moore is instantly recognizable and is a symbol of the modern art movement of the twentieth century. His work can be seen in many public spaces as well as in galleries and private collections.**

new wealth created a new class of patrons of the arts. Middle class factory owners, merchants, and business people had lots of money and collected works of art, but they were largely uneducated in the arts and were criticized for lacking taste.

The painter William Morris, in a reaction to the Industrial Revolution, led a revival movement of individual craftsmanship and design in the 1860s. In architecture, a nostalgic movement led to a comeback for the Gothic style and classical Greek forms.

The founding of the Halle Orchestra in Manchester was part of a music revival in England, and the composer Edward Elgar composed his famous *Pomp and Circumstance* marches. Gilbert and Sullivan's jolly operettas were enjoyed by those who visited the music halls.

The beginning of the twentieth century was known as the Edwardian Era, because Edward VII came briefly to the throne. The music hall was still popular, but in 1906, the first movie theater opened. Gradually, movies put the music halls out of business. Charlie Chaplin was the first British movie star. Music lovers still went to concerts, but they could also listen to singers on a new invention, the gramophone. Most middle class homes had a piano.

World War I horrified and yet inspired many. Frederick Delius, Ralph Vaughan Williams, Sir William Walton, Gustav Holst, and Edward Elgar revived English traditions in music. In the 1920s, dance halls where couples could dance the Charleston and listen to jazz music were popular.

In the 1930s, Modernist ideas affected architecture. Buildings were constructed of concrete, steel, and glass. New buildings were functional, that is they looked appropriate to the job they were supposed to do. Music, especially opera and ballet, was brought by radio into the homes of everyone, including people who could not afford to go to concerts and performances.

After World War II, there was a decline in the film industry, but the movies made by David Lean and the Ealing studios are considered classics today. Pop music revolutionized the music scene and society itself. Groups such as the Beatles and the Rolling Stones gained worldwide fame. Public interest in art is served by excellent art galleries and museums for which England and the whole of Britain are famous. The Arts Council of Great Britain, established in 1946, has also helped to develop and improve the understanding of the arts and increase public access to them.

Above: **The composer Edward Elgar. His work reflected the prosperous England of the early 1900s, and he is credited with leading the re-emergence of English classical music in the twentieth century.**

Leisure and Festivals

It would be impossible to list all the hobbies and leisure time interests of the English, but some stand out.

"England is a nation of gardeners" goes a saying, and enormous amounts of time, energy, and money are poured into gardening every spring and summer. Lots of rain and encouragement produce huge masses of colorful flowers and fruit in almost every front garden.

TRADITIONAL CELEBRATIONS

Many celebrations and festivals have their origins in the political or religious history of England. Guy Fawkes Night and May Day are two examples.

(*A Closer Look, page 68*)

Left: Punch and Judy shows date back to the 1600s in England. Whether he is played by a puppet or an actor, Punch is usually portrayed as a nasty, foolish clown who always gets what he deserves in the end.

Reading and Television

With one of the world's highest literacy rates, it is not surprising that a popular English activity is reading. British libraries lend on average ten books a year for every person in the country.

The most popular activity in Britain is watching television! News, documentaries, police dramas, and comedies are all represented, either on the public, tax-supported, British Broadcasting Corporation (BBC) or on commercial channels.

Outdoor Activities

Sports and outdoor activities are popular among people of all ages. The British Field Sports Society, dedicated to the "traditional countryside interests" of hunting and fishing, claims these activities are enjoyed by five million people.

One of the oddest British hobbies is "trainspotting," in which people simply ride or watch trains. Some like to concentrate on certain kinds of trains, while others are more concerned with trains in a particular area. Experienced trainspotters claim to be able to identify trains according to their whistles and by the sounds the train's wheels make on the tracks!

Above: Watching television — a favorite pastime of English children. The average person watches twenty-four hours of television a week, over three hours a day.

CONKERS

Most British children enjoy conkers, a game played with horse chestnuts and string. Players tie the string to their chestnut and try to smash their opponents' with them.

Sports

Sports have always been popular in England, and many of the sports and games played today were developed or invented over the last two hundred years.

Soccer, the most popular sport in England, is played by the most people, especially the young. At the top level, the sport is professional, with the best players earning millions of dollars. After school and on the weekend, children play soccer informally with their friends and formally in organized competitions. People all over the world follow English soccer teams.

WIMBLEDON

The Wimbledon tennis tournament is the most famous in the world. It is the only major tennis competition still played on grass.
(*A Closer Look, page 73*)

Cricket is considered the most English of games and is played throughout the world, particularly in former British colonies. There are eleven players on a cricket team. Two teams play against each other on a large grass field. The rules are complicated. The object of the game is to score runs by hitting a hard red ball with a straight bat made of willow wood. England plays a series of cricket matches called "test matches" against other countries.

The game known as Rugby was developed at Rugby School in England. According to legend, someone called William Webb

Above: **Rowing is a sport often associated with English universities. England has a strong record in Olympic rowing events.**

Ellis got tired of kicking the ball during a soccer game, so he picked it up and ran with it. A Rugby Union team consists of fifteen players who are organized into a front and back row. As in American football, the object of the game is to carry or kick the ball until it is placed over a line at the end of the field, thus scoring a "try" and earning points.

These days, with more money and more leisure hours, many people enjoy a variety of pastimes such as hiking, bicycling, rock climbing, mountaineering, fishing, and skiing. Sports such as shooting and fox hunting, although still done today, have become

Below: **Rugby Union is a rough and tumble form of football played at all levels from school to international competitions. It tends to be played more in the south of England and often at private schools and universities.**

less popular because many people object to their violence. Golf, which originated in Scotland, is played throughout England, and England has many top class golfers who play in world professional competitions. Hockey is played by men and women, and British hockey teams are often medal winners at the Olympic Games and other world competitions. England has had considerable success in track and field events, and athletes such as Sebastian Coe, Steve Ovett, Steve Cram, and Sally Gunner have achieved Olympic and world medals and records.

SOCCER: THE NATIONAL SPORT

Soccer is the national sport and is watched and played by millions of people all over England.
(A Closer look, page 62)

Halloween

The American celebration of Halloween actually began as a Celtic New Year's Eve called Samhain. On this night, the ancient Celts believed that the dead returned to life, along with many powerful spirits. Bonfires were burned to keep them at bay! The Christian Church tried to tame this wild and frightening celebration by making a holy day out of the following day, which is still known as All Saints or All Hallows. The night before then came to be called All Hallow Evening or "Hallowe'en." Trick-or-treating has its origin in the children's tradition of making mischief on this night.

Easter

The Easter season really begins with Lent, a forty-day period in which Christians are expected to give up something they like. Shrove Tuesday is the last Tuesday before Lent and is often celebrated in England as "Pancake Day." Since Lent is a time of self-denial and lean eating, people traditionally tried to use up all the leftover fat or grease in the house on Shrove Tuesday. They did this by making pancakes and still have pancake races.

Below: **Morris dance teams come out to perform for all sorts of occasions. There are many different morris dance traditions in England. The dancers below are carrying sticks and wearing bells around their legs. Other teams may wave hankies as they dance.**

Guy Fawkes Night

On November 5, 1605, Guy Fawkes and a band of fanatics tried unsuccessfully to blow up parliament. Soon bonfires were lit across London to celebrate the discovery of the Gunpowder Plot, as it became known. To this day, a dummy of Fawkes, called a "guy," is burned. It is dressed in a coat, waistcoat, and trousers, with a colorful mask and holds a lantern in one hand and matches in the other. A "penny for the guy" is collected, and the money is often used to buy fireworks. This noisy celebration traveled to the United States, where it was called Pope's Day. George Washington suggested that people use their fireworks on the Fourth of July instead, which is how the custom became associated with American Independence Day.

Morris Dancing

Morris dancing is an ancient English custom. Dancers perform at May Day and Boxing Day, as well as at regional festivals, such as harvest festivals, throughout the country.

Below: **A huge Guy Fawkes night bonfire.**

Food

Whereas the French and Italians are famous for their cuisine, English food is not considered by critics to be in the same league. Many English people would say this is unfair, and there is a lot of English food too good to miss!

Fast food is not new to England. Fish and chips is a traditional English fast food. Fish is eaten with vinegar or tomato sauce, and often with pickled onions and gherkins on the side. Recent immigration trends have resulted in Indian curry, Middle East kebabs, and Chinese take-out foods competing with the "chippies," or fish and chip shops, for the fast food dollar.

Eating at pubs, especially at lunch time, is a common social activity. Pubs sell alcohol as well as food and have been a part of English life for hundreds of years. In small villages, the pub is often the main social gathering place. Traditional pub food includes "bangers and mash," which is a dish of sausages, mashed potatoes, and gravy, and "ploughman's lunch," a piece of cheese, bread and butter, pickled onion, chutney, or pickles.

Sunday lunch is an English tradition. The family sits down to a meal consisting of a roast meat, usually beef, with Yorkshire pudding and gravy, and baked and boiled vegetables. Yorkshire pudding is made of flour, eggs, and milk beaten into a batter then cooked in fat from the meat in a very hot oven.

Many English food items are named after the region where they were first made. England has excellent cheeses named after counties. These include Cheddar and Stilton. Devonshire is famous for its clotted cream, and a Devonshire tea is a light meal of scones, jam, cream, and tea.

The English have always enjoyed meat pies. In the old days, rabbits, pigeons, and game birds such as pheasant and partridge were the fillings in pies. These days, steak, kidney, chicken, and pork are more popular.

Some dishes have strange names. "Spotted dick" is the name of a pudding. It is made from animal fat, eggs, flour, and raisins. The ingredients are mixed together, shaped into a roll and steamed. "Toad-in-the-hole" is made from sausages cooked in batter. "Bubble and squeak" is a dish of leftover mashed potatoes and any other vegetables all mashed together and fried in butter.

Above: **The famous English meal of fish and chips. Every town has at least one fish and chip shop known as "the chippy."**

Opposite: **Children enjoying their school lunch. English children usually have a hot meal provided by their school at low cost. Typical meals are fish "fingers," baked beans, sausages, potatoes, or macaroni cheese. Steamed pudding, custard, and jelly are popular desserts. Recently, nutritionists have pointed out that these meals are often high in unhealthy salt, fat, and sugar. So school meals are changing, with more fresh fruit and vegetarian food.**

CADBURY WORLD

Cadbury's chocolate is enjoyed by people all over the world, but the story of the Cadbury family and their social efforts is less well known.
(A Closer Look, page 44)

A CLOSER LOOK AT ENGLAND

For a small place, England is densely packed, with people and their multitude of activities, with history and the stories that still have an impact on English and international life today, with an often rain-drenched landscape of mountains, chalk cliffs, lakes, rivers, canals, and seacoast.

The English themselves are a study in contrasts. With animals, they are often kindness itself, but sports such as fox hunting remain a part of English life. Some enjoy chocolate and "watching telly" (television), although others prefer to play soccer or spend the day watching trains go past.

This section will give you a closer look at England and the English people. Much information will be as familiar as your next-door neighbors, or as surprising as the taste of vinegar on French fries.

Opposite: **Students at Cambridge bicycling and enjoying the historic grounds of the university.**

Below: **Stourhead House in Wiltshire, west of London. This beautiful old home is cared for by the National Trust, a charity dedicated to preserving places of historic interest and natural beauty.**

Cadbury World

Cadbury World, located just outside Birmingham, is a theme park dedicated to one of the world's favorite treats — chocolate. The Cadbury Factory Packaging Plant is open to visitors for fragrant, chocolate-soaked tours every day except company holidays.

The Cadbury Fantasy Factory features rides and slides in the shape of Cadbury's candies, where children can build up an appetite for chocolate and goodies of all kinds. Visitors can learn how chocolate was made by John Cadbury and later his sons George and Richard, who developed the now-famous Dairy Milk chocolate bar.

Above: **An early advertisement for Cadbury's Cocoa. The hot chocolate drink sold by Cadbury's was the foundation of their business empire.**

How Did Cadbury's Begin?

Although Cadbury World might seem to be dedicated to chocolate and fun times, its early history was a story of social consciousness.

John Cadbury was a Quaker, part of a Christian group opposed to the drinking of alcohol in any form. As an alternative to bars and pubs, in 1824 he opened a chocolate shop in Birmingham serving hot chocolate — "a most nutritious beverage." Success came quickly, and he soon had to rent a small factory and then a larger one to keep up with the tremendous demand for this drink. His sons, George and Richard, carried on the business as well as his good works.

George Cadbury was involved in the Adult School Movement, which tried to educate the poor. While visiting his students in central Birmingham, he became aware of the terrible conditions under which they and their families lived and set out to do something to help.

The Move to Bournville

The Cadbury brothers decided to move their entire operation into the green belt around the city of Birmingham. They bought part of a country estate, named it Bournville, and built a village. In addition to moving their factory, the brothers also moved their workers to Bournville, building homes, schools, churches, and even a hospital for them. Fresh air and light replaced the darkness and mud of Birmingham.

To preserve the village for future generations, the Bournville Village Trust was formed and is still in operation today. It is praised as an early example of English town planning.

Chocolate and Slavery

The Quakers were outspoken opponents of the practice of slavery. Unfortunately, slave labor was used in the cultivation of cacao trees, used to make chocolate. In the early 1900s, when the Cadburys and other English chocolate makers became aware of the way in which slaves were forced to work on cocoa plantations, they organized a successful voluntary boycott of cocoa grown in such places. In addition, they gathered support for the boycott from chocolate companies in the United States and Germany.

While people do not need to know the history of Cadbury's chocolate to enjoy a visit to Cadbury World, or even to bite into a bar of Cadbury's chocolate, they might be happy to know that Cadbury's was a business that tried to feed hearts and minds as well as stomachs.

Below: The poorhouses of nineteenth-century England inspired the Cadbury family to provide a better living and working environment for their workers. Poor sanitation and a lack of light and ventilation, combined with the fact that many streets had no drainage, meant the air was foul with the smell of garbage and sewage. In such a squalid environment, hope for a bright future died early, and crime and other social problems emerged.

Canals

A look at some maps of England will show that it is crisscrossed by a web of blue lines. Many of these lines are rivers, but even more are canals, a system of transportation that represents an achievement of human labor and engineering genius.

 The earliest canal was cut in 1571; by 1805, an additional 3,000 miles (4,800 km) had been added to the system. Canals provided a door-to-door service between coal mines, factories and mills, and the cities.

What Kinds of Canals Are There?

There are four types of canals. The first type is the biggest, designed to take seagoing ships. The second type is the mainline canal, found in the East Midlands, Lancashire, and Cheshire. These canals are not as wide, only about 14 feet (4.5 m) across. The third type of canal is actually narrower still and is called, appropriately, a narrow-canal — a mere 7 feet (2 m) wide. The last type of canal is the tub-boat canal, which took long, narrow barges on streams only five feet (1.5 m) across.

Below: Vacationers wishing to take a long, slow look at the English countryside can do so on brightly refurbished narrow-boats. A canal trip gives visitors a look at a way of life that has long since disappeared and a chance to see first-hand the mechanical means by which water moved the fortunes of nineteenth century England.

Although the Romans built an excellent system of roads in Britain, these were not well maintained. Until the eighteenth century, therefore, water was used far more often for transportation.

Left: Locks were required to move vessels from one water level to another. A system of locks, like the one shown here, was built enabling barges to move from one water level to another. This allowed them to operate even in hilly areas.

Life on the Barges

Often, entire families lived on these barges, or narrowboats. The work was hard and the hours were long, with all members of the family helping to steer and sometimes pull the boat out of the water. Cold weather and pouring rain did not stop the barge or its crew from delivering their cargo. A valued member of the work-team was the horse, which pulled the boat along, trudging slowly along the banks of the canals.

Fossil Fuels vs Nuclear Power

Most of the electricity in England is generated by power stations that use traditional energy sources — coal, oil, and gas. These fuels are made from ancient animal and plant remains, which formed fossils under the earth millions of years ago. Most of the oil and gas is found in the North Sea off the coast of Scotland.

Power stations using fossil fuels produce harmful waste products such as smoke and gases that harm people's health and the environment. Some of the gases damage the leaves of nearby trees. Others mix with water droplets forming harmful substances called acids. These acids can be carried by the wind for a long way before falling as acid rain or snow. Today, rain in Europe has eighty times more acid in it than in 1950. Acid rain makes trees weak so insects and disease kill them more easily. Rivers and lakes become more acidic and polluted, and animal life dies.

Since World War II, the government has considered other ways of generating power. One alternative is nuclear power. About a quarter of England's electricity is produced by nuclear power stations. Nuclear power is a controversial issue in England and other parts of the world. Those supporting nuclear power say the production is cleaner than that of fossil fuels and does not use precious resources from the earth. Those who disapprove say that nuclear power production is expensive and hazardous. Waste produced at nuclear power stations is difficult to get rid of because it is radioactive and therefore dangerous.

In 1957, Windscale, a nuclear reactor in Cumbria, caught fire and burned for sixteen hours, releasing radioactive materials into the air. Surveys show that the rate of cancer in people who lived close to the reactor at that time is higher than average. Studies of the milk from cows in the area found the milk contained radioactivity well above the safe limits. This milk had to be destroyed.

Windscale was renamed Sellafield in 1971 when the nuclear agencies were reorganized. In 1997, antinuclear groups in England and elsewhere used the station's thirtieth anniversary to publicize the dangers of nuclear energy.

Above: **England has large coal reserves, but many coal miners face an uncertain future as alternative energy sources are developed.**

Opposite: **Although nuclear energy is considered a "clean" power source, many people protest its use because of the dangers posed by nuclear accidents and waste disposal. This rally was held in opposition to the Sellafield nuclear reactor.**

The Lake District

The Lake District in the northwest forms England's largest national park. Famous for its varied scenery, the park sees eighteen million visitors every year, enjoying the lakes, mountains, and villages. People boat and fish in the sixteen lakes. The poet William Wordsworth, who lived in the district for many years, also recommended the view from the top of Scafell Pike, England's highest mountain. Visitors stay in pretty villages such as Grasmere, a cluster of gray stone houses next to the babbling River Rothay, or at Ambelside, which has a sports festival every August.

Below: **Long ago, the Lake District area was a huge dome, much higher than Scafell Pike. Water and glaciers during the ice ages eroded the land and carved valleys. When the glaciers melted, they left deposits of sediment, which trapped water and formed these lakes.**

The Lake District is also well known for the famous people, especially poets and painters, who have lived and visited there in the last two hundred years. Arthur Ransome wrote of children on vacation, sailing and having adventures in the Lake District, in his children's classic *Swallows and Amazons* and in other books in the series. The children's writer Beatrix Potter spent nearly forty years in the district. Charlotte Brontë was the guest of writer Harriet Martineau in 1850.

Beatrix Potter

Beatrix Potter, born in 1866, was a lonely town child who loved nature and painting, and wanted to live in the country. A patient observer of small animals, her first and possibly most famous story, "Peter Rabbit," was sent in a letter to a friend's child. Over a period of twelve years, she created a number of small books about animals for children that are still popular today. These animals are like people: they talk, wear clothes, visit each other, and have a family life.

In 1905, she moved to Near Sawrey in the Lake District and shortly after wrote what many people feel is her best book, *The Tale of Samuel Whiskers*. She married a local lawyer named Heelis, and a gallery showing many of Potter's book illustrations now occupies the office once used by her husband in the village of Hawkshead.

Above: **Donald Campbell, an English national hero, set a world water-speed record in 1955 on a lake named Ullswater. On January 4, 1967, on Coniston Water, he tried to set a new record, but his jet-powered boat, *Bluebird*, crashed, and he was killed.**

Left: **Beatrix Potter loved the Lake District and bought large areas of land. When she died in 1943, she bequeathed this land to the National Trust. Today, fans of Potter visit her home, "Hill Top," which is cared for by the Trust. Potter was a keen naturalist and conservationist long before such views became fashionable.**

Love for Animals

The English are a nation of pet lovers. The Queen has her beloved corgis, Princess Anne her horses, and others have their dogs, cats, hamsters, gerbils, guinea pigs, goldfish, and almost any other kind of creature. A few examples of the English kindness to animals tell a lot about their character.

Ducks on Downing Street

Number 10 Downing Street is a very famous London address, because it is the home of the British prime minister. Not long ago, it was the scene of an unusual rescue. A duck and her sixteen ducklings decided to leave their pond in St. James' Park and waddled over to the nearby Horseguards Parade. They crossed a busy road single-file, amid loud screeching of car brakes, but without mishap. From there they walked around the Foreign Office up to Downing Street. Avoiding the sidewalk but staying in

Below: **London police officers ensuring the safety of the Downing Street ducks. According to one report, "It took some time before the ducks put the down back into Downing Street."**

the center of the street, they passed the prime minister's house and started to cross a six-lane road. The policemen guarding the house abandoned their posts in a frantic rush to scoop up the wandering ducklings in their police helmets.

Eventually the ducklings were all captured, much against their will. A park warden came later to collect them.

A Hedgehog Hospital at Prickly Ball Farm

Prickly Ball Farm is a small farm in the Devon countryside and runs what is possibly the only hedgehog hospital open to the public. Hedgehogs are smaller, more cuddly versions of the familiar porcupine and have become an unofficial mascot for responsible driving.

Why a hedgehog hospital? In fact, what appears to be a charming idea for young visitors is a result of roads being built across natural hedgehog habitats. Not knowing the dangers of traffic, hedgehogs are often hit by cars, which have become a major cause of hedgehog deaths. Staff at Prickly Ball Farm tend to injured hedgehogs and prepare them for a return to the wild. In addition, visitors learn how to keep their own backyards safer for wild animals.

Top: Dog owners race their hounds to see which is the fastest.

Above: Cats are a favorite household pet in many families.

Oxford and Cambridge Universities

England's oldest and most prestigious universities, Oxford and Cambridge, began as gatherings of scholars who lived and studied together in the twelfth century. These small communities formed colleges, the oldest probably being University College, Oxford (1249) and Merton College, also in Oxford (1264).

Left: The entrance to King's College at Cambridge. Although they follow many old traditions, these schools are also very much part of the modern educational system. Students at Oxford and Cambridge have access to modern technology as well as some of the finest libraries and museums in the world. The Bodleian Library at Oxford, for example, contains over six million books, in dozens of languages, with online search services and facilities for accessing information in CD-ROMs and remote databases.

The ancient tutorial system is still the backbone of education at Oxford and Cambridge. Students meet with their tutors once a week, usually in a one-on-one arrangement, although small groups may be set up and are given a problem to solve or an area of study. They then work independently and report back a week later, either with an essay on the subject or perhaps a short presentation.

Examinations at the end of the third year determine whether the student will graduate, and students may also have to write research papers.

Stuck in the Past, or Ready for the Future?

Oxford and Cambridge have been criticized as being "elitist" and not preparing students for practical, "real world" concerns. Others feel that too much money is invested in the education of too few students and that the money ought to be shared more fairly among all students instead of just a select group.

Today, companies are invited to make donations to the universities or to pay for books or equipment. The discipline, independence, and research skills students learn in tutorial education are considered very desirable in their future jobs.

Top: A tutorial in progress. Students are encouraged to learn by questioning their tutors and through individual study.

Above: Most students live on campus in single rooms at their colleges — some of the rooms may be six hundred years old.

Protecting Nature

Cultivation of land in England has been going on since ancient times, and one result is that there are no longer vast forests or wilderness areas. Today, only about 7 percent of the land is forested. However, conservation of their natural heritage, both land and wildlife, is very important to the English.

Environmental Groups

The Nature Conservancy Council works to protect wildlife habitats and has saved some of the last refuges of wild animals and birds in England. Marine conservation is also important, and the National Marine Nature Reserves have been set up to protect the coastal areas. By far the largest owner of nature reserves in Britain is the National Trust, which owns nearly half a million acres (200,000 hectares) of land in nature reserves and areas of countryside. The trust also controls over 400 miles (640 km) of coastline.

Below: **The deciduous forests that once covered England have mostly been cleared for farming. Today, hedgerows, strips of trees through farm-land, are considered an important and beautiful feature of the English countryside. They are abundantly populated with birds and small animals.**

The Hedgerow

A unique feature of the English landscape is the hedgerow. Hedgerows are long strips of trees and bushes originally planted as long ago as the Middle Ages for the purpose of enclosing farmland. Later, during the Industrial Revolution and the growth of the wool trade, they were an essential means of keeping sheep penned in. Today, they are valued for the many birds and small animals that live in them. Unfortunately, many miles of hedgerows have already been lost to development and large scale agricultural interests, which use large, open parcels of land rather than smaller enclosed areas. The English have responded to these threats with projects that try to educate people about the value of hedgerows and encourage their responsible management.

Long Distance Trails

The English enjoy hiking, and there are some 105,000 miles (168,000 km) of footpaths, bridleways, and byways in England, some of which date back to Roman times and earlier. The system of long distance trails stretches the length and width of the country and is an important source of recreation for families and serious walkers.

Above: **Students sometimes take field trips to gain first-hand knowledge of the environment.**

Robin Hood

Was There a Real Robin Hood?

According to legend, Robin Hood was an outlaw who committed the crime of poaching, or hunting illegally, in the king's forest. Another story says that he fled to Sherwood Forest as a young man when his father was killed and his house burned down. In order to avoid his deadly enemy, the Sheriff of Nottingham, Robin Hood retreated to the forest.

The common people benefited from Robin's good heart, for he never kept the goods and gold he stole but instead gave them to the poor. Despite his crimes, Robin stayed loyal to the king, Richard I, called Richard the Lionheart (who reigned from 1189–1199). While Richard was off fighting in the Crusades or in France, his brother John repeatedly abused power by heavily taxing everyone.

Below: **This statue of the legendary Robin Hood stands in front of Nottingham Castle.**

Robin Hood is said to have died as an old man in a priory in Yorkshire, where his aunt (or some say Maid Marian) was a nun. When Robin realized he was dying, he summoned Little John from the forest. Robin asked for his bow, then fired an arrow through the window, saying that he should be buried where the arrow landed. Nearby, one can see Robin Hood's grave and the epitaph on his gravestone:

> *Here underneath this little stone*
> *Lies Robert Earl of Huntington*
> *Never archer was as he so good*
> *And people called him Robin Hood.*
> *Such outlaws as he and his men*
> *Will England never see again.*

However, most scholars do not believe this place really marks Robin Hood's grave because the epitaph is written in a style that belongs more to eighteenth century English, long after Robin Hood's time. Prince John eventually died from overeating, perhaps a fitting death. Richard was killed in France, but it is Robin Hood whose name we remember.

Above: **Robin Hood's capture by the Sheriff of Nottingham was only temporary. His tricks and disguises to rob or cheat the rich out of their money made him a popular figure in English folklore, where songs and plays about him have been performed since the thirteenth century. Many of the legends celebrate his unequalled skill in archery and his daring escapes from the clutches of Prince John and the Sheriff of Nottingham.**

Sir Francis Drake:
Pirate or Dragon?

Francis Drake was born in Tavistock, Devonshire, and went to sea as a boy. On one voyage, he was sailing along Mexico's east coast when his ship was attacked by Spaniards. Stripped of all he owned and demoralized by the Spaniards' cruelty to their English prisoners, Drake vowed revenge. During his journey around the world, beginning in 1577, Drake attacked Spanish settlements along the coasts of Chile and Peru and treasure-laden Spanish ships heading north to Panama. Laden with precious cargo, he returned

Left: **The Spanish called Sir Francis Drake *El Draque*, "The Dragon," and he was their great enemy. His first voyage was on a slave ship to Guinea, on the west coast of Africa, and eventually he commanded his own ship. On several of his voyages, he returned to the New World to sack Spanish towns and raid Spanish ships. Each time, he returned to Queen Elizabeth's court with new treasure. Although we would call his actions piracy today, to the English, he was a triumphant hero.**

to England. He was given a rousing welcome by Queen Elizabeth I, who even accepted an invitation to dinner on board Drake's ship. Risking the anger of Spain, Elizabeth knighted Drake.

Queen Elizabeth I (who reigned from 1558–1603) was in conflict with the Spanish during this time. Having rejected Catholicism during the reign of Henry VIII, the English monarchy had been opposed and plotted against by Catholic Spain for twenty years. Queen Elizabeth also wanted to end the Spanish monopoly on trade in the Pacific. For this reason, she secretly sent Drake on his greatest voyage of all, a trip around the world to find new trading routes, in his ship, the *Golden Hind*.

The Last Journey

In January 1596, near the Panama coast, Drake became ill and died. He died as he lived, on board ship and harassing the Spanish. Whether he is considered a pirate or, more politely, a "privateer," there can be no doubt that Sir Francis Drake's voyages brought the English closer to the sea and the seafaring for which they later became famous.

Above: **Conflict with Spain, long simmering, finally burst into war in 1585. Sir Francis Drake, now vice-admiral of the English navy, played a major part in the Spanish defeat. In 1587, Drake raided the Spanish port of Cádiz, destroying thirty-eight Spanish ships that were to have become part of the Spanish Armada preparing to attack England.**

Soccer: The National Sport

The game soccer, called football in England, is very popular. Children play soccer at school and in weekend competitions. Men play the game at professional and amateur levels. There are amateur competitions for women, too. As well as playing soccer, people enjoy watching the games live and on television. The spectators often wear scarves and caps with their team's colors.

A soccer team has eleven players. Two teams play against each other on a large grassy area called a pitch. The object of the game is to kick the ball into the opposing team's goal. Except for

Left: **Arsenal's Ian Wright (in red) clashes with Wimbledon's Dean Blackwell during their London Derby at Selhurst Park. The very best players are media celebrities and millionaires, and loyal fans spend a lot of money on club merchandise associated with their favorite player. When the team Newcastle United paid fifteen million pounds as a transfer fee for the player Alan Shearer, within a week, five million pounds worth of shirts with Shearer's name on them were sold.**

the goalkeeper, players are not allowed to touch the ball with their hands. They mainly use their feet to kick the ball, although sometimes they use their heads to push the ball. Goalkeepers, one for each team, stand in front of the goal and try to stop the ball from going into the goal by catching the ball in their hands, kicking it with their feet, or blocking it with their bodies.

The Football League Championship was formed in 1888 with twelve teams. The League now has over seventy teams divided into three divisions: first, second, and third. In 1992, the best teams from the first division formed a premier league. English football teams also play against other European clubs for the Union of European Football Associations (UEFA) Cup.

England's proudest moment came when the team representing England won the World Cup in 1966. England defeated Germany by a score of 4–2 after extra time, at Wembley Stadium. The captain of the team was Bobby Charlton. One player, Geoff Hurst, scored three successive goals to give England the victory.

Above: **Fulham turned into a sea of blue and yellow as Chelsea fans lined the streets to welcome home their 1997 FA (Football Association) Cup winning team. Chelsea beat Middlesbrough at Wembley to win the prized trophy.**

Stonehenge

Situated near Salisbury in a part of southern England called Wiltshire, Stonehenge is a group of large standing stones. What we see today is only a small part of an earth and stone complex that was built between 3,000 and 1,000 B.C. Although Stone Age people started it, most of the longer second stage of building was done by a Bronze Age group, the Beaker Folk, who moved to England from eastern Europe. Their interesting name comes from the clay mugs they made and buried with their dead. Later building at the site was completed by a more advanced society called the Wessex culture.

Unfortunately, much of the original stone was later used as building materials by local people so not much remains of this great monument. The present structure is relatively small and consists of four concentric groups of stones. The outside group is a circle and has large sandstone blocks with lintels known as sarsen stones. Inside this circle is a smaller circle made up of bluestones, and inside this stand five stones arranged in the shape of a horseshoe. Then there is a smaller horseshoe of bluestones with a slab of sandstone like an altar in the middle.

Below: **Archaeologists are not sure why such time and effort was spent on building Stonehenge. Perhaps it was a temple of sun worship or sacrifice, a place for meetings, ceremonial gatherings, or astronomical study, or even a palace.**

There were no cranes or trucks to move such large stones in ancient times, so a large number of people must have toiled over hundreds of years. Thousands of people worked all their lives on the construction of Stonehenge and then left the task to their descendants to finish.

Some of the stones are from the Prescelly Mountains in Wales, 150 miles (240 km) away. How did they move them? Some archaeologists believe that land transportation was kept to a minimum by floating the stones on rafts along the coast, up the Bristol Channel, and up the Avon and Frome rivers. On land, the stones could have been put on wooden rollers and slowly moved across the countryside.

Above: A large, artificial pyramid-shaped hill, Sidbury Hill in Wiltshire covers over 5 acres (2 hectares). Archaeologists think it was a barrow, an earthen burial mound built for an important person, possibly the chief who ordered the building of the Avebury monument.

Other Ancient Monuments in England

The village of Avebury, near Marlborough in Wiltshire, stands in the middle of a stone circle built by the Beaker Folk around 2,500 B.C., earlier than Stonehenge. This largest known megalithic circle has stones that are smaller than those at Stonehenge, but the circle is much wider and the construction is more complex.

The Rollright Stones are the third most important stone circle after Stonehenge and Avebury. Legend says these stones are a king and his army frozen by a witch's curse.

Suffragettes

Women can now vote and run for office in England, but that was not always so. In the early twentieth century, women campaigning for women's suffrage, that is the right to vote, were labeled suffragettes. Before the nineteenth century, girls were considered to be intellectually inferior to boys. Although Elizabeth Blackwell graduated in 1849 as the world's first trained, registered woman doctor, there was still a lot of pressure against girls being educated in the same way as boys.

The Right to Vote

Despite some gains made in the law and education, and although most men in England could vote, a number of bills promising English women the vote were repeatedly defeated in parliament.

The suffragettes, led by Emmeline Pankhurst, seeing that quiet methods of protest had failed, became more aggressive.

Below, left: **Suffragettes chained themselves to fences in front of government buildings to protest their lack of rights.**

Below, right: **Large rallies to encourage the support of the public were held in the early 1900s. The government responded with brutal suppression, imprisoning many suffragettes. When the women went on hunger strikes, some nearly died and those in prison were force-fed.**

Left: Emily Davies was a woman who worked to reform the higher education of women. Due to her efforts in the late nineteenth century, girls were allowed to take university entrance exams with boys, and women started attending universities in greater numbers. In 1873, Girton College, the first residence for women students at Cambridge University, was set up with Emily Davies as its head. The struggle for sexual equality continues today. Here, women are protesting against the lower rates of pay for women compared to men.

They chained themselves to railings outside important government buildings, damaged property, detonated bombs, cut telephone lines, disrupted political meetings, harassed politicians, and organized mass marches. In 1913 Emily Davidson, in a tragic protest at a race meeting, threw herself under a galloping racehorse owned by the king.

World War I intervened. The suffragettes paused in their campaign and encouraged women to help the war effort by working in traditionally male jobs in industry and agriculture. This work received much praise, and public attitudes changed. In 1918, the Representation of the People Act allowed married women, women property owners, and graduate women over thirty to vote. It was not until 1928, however, that all women over twenty-one could vote. Today, men and women can vote at age eighteen.

Traditional Celebrations

Many of England's traditional celebrations are based on ancient pagan beliefs that were part of people's lives before the coming of Christianity. Nowadays, the English decorate the house with evergreen boughs to celebrate Christmas, but this custom was originally practiced by people as a fertility rite. Other celebrations familiar to us also have their origins in the past and have been a part of life in England for thousands of years.

Left: **English children enjoy Easter egg hunts and tales of the Easter bunny. They also enjoy egg rolling — children roll eggs down a hill until they are cracked, and then eat them. Mumming, or performing the Easter story, is part of the season's celebrations in many rural parts of England.**

Traditional Easter Celebrations

Although we now celebrate Easter as a Christian holiday, it had its origins in a spring festival held in Anglo-Saxon times in honor of *Eostre* (EE-struh), the goddess of dawn.

Two peculiar customs, the Hare-Pie Scramble and Bottle-kicking, are observed on Easter Monday in Leicestershire (less-tuh-SHEAR) and nowhere else. No one knows how they started, but they have a long history, dating back to medieval times and are considered too much fun to give up!

May Day

May Day was the first day of the summer according to the old Celtic calendar and is still celebrated with maypole dancing and sometimes the arrival of a procession led by a hobby horse. The hobby horse is played by someone in an elaborate costume wearing a mock horse's head. After marching up and down the streets during the day, the hobby horse is ritually "killed" and born again, linking the modern age with ancient fertility rites.

Above: **The maypole dance is performed by a group of dancers, each holding a colored ribbon attached to a pole about 10 feet (3 m) tall. As the dancers weave in and out, the ribbons are woven in a pattern around the pole.**

"The Troubles"

The problems between the Irish and English go back many centuries. Conflict between the primarily Catholic Irish and the Protestant English and Scottish led up to the first Irish rebellion, during the reign of Elizabeth I (1558–1603). Despite help from their Catholic ally Spain, the Irish were completely defeated. Elizabeth's successor, James I, treated Ireland as a colony and moved thousands of Scots to Ulster, or northern Ireland, pushing the native Irish people out.

The execution of Charles I and the resulting takeover of the country by Cromwell in 1648 saw another Irish rebellion, again, ruthlessly crushed. By 1653, Ulster was completely in the hands of the Protestants.

Below: **Acts of terrorism have been used by both sides to draw attention to their cause. The problems between the Irish and the English are, in part, based on religious differences. The Irish were converted to Catholicism at the beginning of the fifth century and remain largely Catholic today.**

Left: **By the twentieth century, conditions in Ireland had improved greatly, but strong divisions emerged between north and south. The southerners, traditionally Catholic, began to push for home rule, while those in Ulster, the "Unionists," wished to stay British. British soldiers are stationed in Northern Ireland as peacekeepers, but many feel their presence is the cause of much conflict.**

The Movement for Home Rule

A rebellion in 1916 failed, resulting in the execution of fourteen Irish leaders. This in turn increased the Irish people's support for independence. The Irish revolutionary party, Sinn Féin (SHIN FANE), won most of the seats in a parliamentary election, but they refused to sit in an English parliament and instead set up their own.

In 1920, the Government of Ireland Act resulted in a legal division, so that the six northern counties formed Northern Ireland, with the remainder joining the Irish Free State, which became part of the British Commonwealth. But the Irish were still not content; some wanted complete independence. In 1948, the Irish Free State, or Éire (AYER), left the Commonwealth and renamed itself the Republic of Ireland, and, in 1973 its government was given some control over Irish affairs in Northern Ireland, against the strong protests of the Northern Ireland Protestants.

ROAD TO PEACE?

Recently, there has been strong support for peace in Northern Ireland, and attempts are being made to find a permanent solution to the troubles. In an important peace deal in April 1998, leaders from all sides of the conflict agreed to work toward a compromise that would build closer links between Northern Ireland and Ireland and allow both Catholics and Protestants to work together to run Northern Ireland.

Wimbledon

Although millions of television viewers watch tennis greats playing on center court at Wimbledon, and spectators watch the matches live in seats they have purchased for great sums of money, not many know that Wimbledon's first link with sports was the old fashioned game of croquet. The All England Croquet Club was founded at Wimbledon, a London suburb, in 1868. But the game of croquet proved boring for many and was replaced seven years later by the newer game of tennis. The club changed its name to the All England Lawn Tennis and Croquet Club and the Wimbledon home of international tennis was established.

Lawn tennis sprung from the much older indoor game of "real" or "royal" tennis, and the rules of the new game were not firmly established. A club committee decided it should be played on a measured, rectangular court of grass with certain rules and scoring. The club launched its first competition for men in 1877. The first winner was Spencer Gore. The first women's singles competition was held in 1884 and was won by Maud Watson.

Wimbledon became the first major tennis tournament to admit professionals in 1968. The club made this decision against the advice of the International Lawn Tennis Federation. The men's singles match in that year was won by Rod Laver of Australia and the women's singles by Billie Jean King from the United States.

Since then, the Wimbledon competition has prospered with new sponsorship. Of the four major tennis competitions known as the Grand Slam — the Australian Open, the French Open, the U.S. Open, and Wimbledon, Wimbledon is the only one to be played on the game's original surface, grass. Since World War II, the singles winners have mainly come from the United States, Australia, and Germany.

Wimbledon is one of the sporting and social highlights of the English summer. It is held in the last week of June and the first week of July. Tickets are difficult to obtain, especially for center court and the No. 1 court where the top players usually play. Afternoon tea with strawberries and cream and champagne is a tradition. The royal family has its own area known as the royal box, and the trophies are presented by the Duke or Duchess of Kent. The Duke is the current president of the club.

Above: **Players dress differently today than they did in the past; they also earn a lot more money. The first prize in 1877 was twenty-five pounds, a tiny amount when compared to the thousands offered today. For most of its history, however, Wimbledon was an amateur championship.**

Opposite: **Top tennis players aspire to play and win at Wimbledon. They say no other competition has the special atmosphere Wimbledon has. In 1997, Martina Hingis of Switzerland was the world's top-ranked women's player and the Wimbledon champion.**

RELATIONS WITH NORTH AMERICA

Relations between England (now part of the United Kingdom) and Canada and the United States are firmly cemented by a long shared past. English exploration of the North American continent began in the fifteenth century when John Cabot claimed Newfoundland (in Canada) and parts of what is now the state of Maine (in the United States) for the British Crown. Later, in 1584, Walter Raleigh explored Virginia (also in the United States). Between 1607 and 1700, the English colonies of Virginia, the Carolinas, Georgia, and what is now New England, were settled. Colonial North America was in some ways a place for English settlers to start life over. The Puritans, who arrived in the early 1600s, for example, hoped to "purify" and simplify the Anglican Church. Others came in search of furs, gold, or whales. British trappers and traders also followed the French to Canada to pursue a profitable trade in furs for the Hudson's Bay Company.

Opposite: **The long history of English seafaring still echoes in the many fishing villages along the English coast.**

Left: **In 1620, the *Mayflower* arrived at Cape Cod, Massachusetts, after a month-long voyage from Plymouth in England. It carried Pilgrims seeking a new life free from the constraints of English religious persecution.**

The American Revolution

The English settlers of the new colonies were given the right to self-government, but they were not allowed to control their own trade. In order to pay for war against France, the English parliament imposed heavy taxes on the American colonies. "No taxation without representation" became the battle-cry of the protesting colonists, and parliament responded by repealing some taxes but imposing others. After riots in Boston, parliament repealed the taxes again, only to impose the infamous duty on tea that resulted in the Boston Tea Party of 1773, when crates of tea were thrown into Boston Harbor.

Parliament punished the colonists with the so-called "Intolerable Acts," which restricted people's income and freedoms. Boston Harbor was closed until the tea was paid for and the Massachusetts Charter, which had guaranteed self-government, was virtually repealed. Because Boston was suffering most of the punishment, many revolutionary activities began in that city. In 1770, the Boston Massacre further inflamed the spirits of the colonies against their rulers. The first shots of the American Revolution were fired in Lexington, Massachusetts.

Below: **The Boston Tea Party. In a protest against what they considered unfair taxes, colonists dumped crates of East India tea into Boston Harbor.**

King George III was reigning at this time (1760–1820). He became famous for two things: his madness and losing the American colonies. The state of Georgia in the United States was named after him.

Leaving for Canada

Colonists who remained loyal to the British Crown were called United Empire Loyalists. They left the United States and settled in Nova Scotia, New Brunswick, and Quebec (in Canada). Independent since 1931, the Dominion of Canada became a fully independent country in 1982 when it was granted the right to amend the constitution established under the British North America Act. Many English-speaking Canadians feel considerable loyalty to their British past. The long and largely peaceful relationship shared by Britain and Canada has resulted in ties that are deep and committed. In June 1997, the prime ministers of Britain and Canada met to further develop the relationship through trade, investment, science, technology, defense, and education.

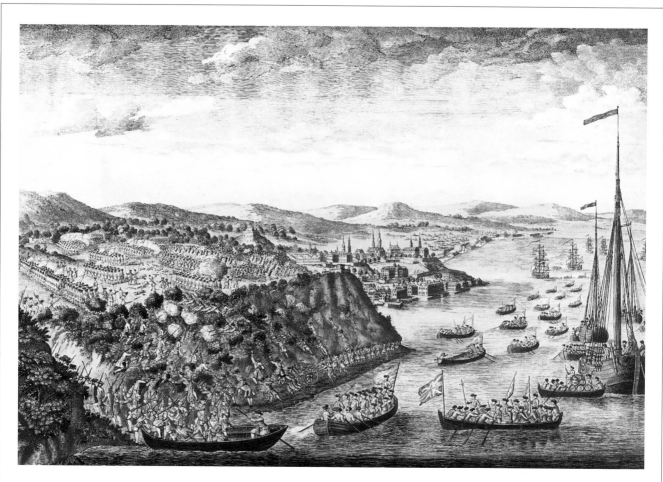

Immigration

Immigration to the New World came in waves. The earliest immigrants, as we have seen, were English colonists, who came in search of a life they could not have in England.

Above: **The taking of Quebec. In 1759, the British took possession of the French colony of Quebec in Canada.**

Beyond religious freedom, the search for a good life was a big attraction. The Virginia colony, for example, was settled by Englishmen who came to buy land, raise tobacco (which had been introduced to Britain by Walter Raleigh years earlier), and generally lead comfortable lives as "country squires," something they would find impossible in England.

A major difference between the English and the Americans was the idea that in North America, a person's value was measured in terms of what he or she could do, while in England, social rank or position was a major factor in the way people viewed each other. For many English, emigration meant opportunity. A person's past could be forgotten, or perhaps conveniently rewritten.

Between 1830 and 1890, thousands of British and Irish settlers came to North America. For the English and Welsh, the difficult working and living conditions brought about by the Industrial Revolution at home became a reason to leave. Long working hours and crowded, unhealthy conditions in the cities caused people, especially the young, to emigrate.

The rich farmland and open spaces of Canada attracted English settlers, but by the late 1800s, the cheap land of the western United States attracted nearly as many Canadians to the United States, so there was no great change in the population in Canada at that time.

English immigrants still arrive in waves on the North American continent. The old economic hardships are largely gone, although some still mention high British taxes as a very good reason to take up residence in the United States! On the whole, Canada retains more of an "English" flavor, especially in places such as Victoria, British Columbia.

Below: **Many of the new settlers were fleeing religious persecution in their own countries. Religion played an important role in the establishment of these early communities, which were based on the Protestant work ethic advocating hard work and the deferment of pleasure.**

North Americans in England

North Americans go to England for many reasons, including business and to study. Because Canada and the United States share a common language and a similar culture with Britain, as well as a strong interest in free trade, there are many business opportunities for North Americans in Britain. American investment in Britain amounts to over $110 billion, and 4,000 American companies are represented there. This means that many Americans find opportunities to live in England. They travel, send their children to the local schools, learn to drive on the left side of the road, play Rugby or soccer instead of American football, and generally experience an English lifestyle.

Left: **American soldiers march through London on their way to a dinner hosted by the British government in appreciation of their efforts during World War II. Military ties between the United States and England have always been strong. As allies, they have fought alongside each other in two world wars and continue to work together as members of NATO.**

The North American military presence in the entire country is still strong. Although it is occasionally protested by local people, it is recognized as important for international security. The 1990 census reported that more than sixteen thousand American military personnel were based in the United Kingdom. Children of American defense personnel based in England go to one of the dozen or so Department of Defense Schools there.

British education is highly regarded by North Americans, and many college and university students try to spend at least one year studying at one of Britain's universities. The recently established Marshall Scholarship will enable American students of excellent academic standing to study for a degree at a British university.

Below: **British prime minister Winston Churchill, President Franklin D. Roosevelt, and Premier Joseph Stalin of the Soviet Union met in Yalta to discuss the division of territories after World War II and lay the foundation of the United Nations.**

Making Peace: The United Nations

In the last days of World War II, leaders from Britain, the United States, and the Soviet Union met in Yalta, Crimea (now the Ukraine), to organize the United Nations. The United Nations Conference on International Organization then opened in San Francisco in April 1945, with delegates from fifty nations who drew up the United Nations Charter. The United Nations' primary goal is world peace.

U.S.–British Relations Today: "Values We Share"

Above: Newly elected prime minister Tony Blair and his wife Cherie met with President and Mrs. Clinton in 1997. Blair's leadership is often compared to that of Bill Clinton's.

Robin Cook, the foreign secretary in Prime Minister Tony Blair's New Labour Party government, wrote an article in the *Washington Post* outlining how Britain hoped to work with the United States in areas of concern that are common to both countries. He wrote first of the need to continue basing Britain's security on NATO (North Atlantic Treaty Organization).

He then mentioned the need to encourage "vigorous free trade and healthy investment flows," in other words, investment by the United States in Britain and by Britain in the United States, for the prosperity of both countries. Concern for the environment was another shared value.

A fourth point related to the protection of human rights; like Americans, the British "are determined not only that their society should remain open and democratic, but also that others should share the freedoms they enjoy."

Cook also wrote of fighting terrorism, reducing nuclear weapons and the use of land mines, and underscored Britain's support of the United Nations and its role in achieving these tasks.

Cultural Connections

Although the people of the United States and Canada are originally from many different countries and ethnic backgrounds, the influence of the English is still considered very strong in both countries' cultures.

The writer and lecturer Alistair Cooke, through his famous Public Broadcasting Service series "Alistair Cooke's America," has been an unofficial ambassador on America's behalf overseas, while giving an English point of view to his American viewers.

Many of England's most talented artists and performers have taken up residence in the United States. Cary Grant, who started as a vaudeville performer called Archie Leach, was a screen idol for many years. Bob Hope, whose Christmas performances for American troops all over the world made him both famous and much loved, is another English transplant. Many British-born actors and actresses successfully switched from stage performances to film; Alec Guinness, who appeared in *Star Wars*, and Laurence Olivier are two. The actress Elizabeth Taylor was a child star whose first major role was in *National Velvet*, a film about a young girl and her horse. Anthony Hopkins, who plays serial killers and elegant butlers with equal ease, is another British actor whose popularity has skyrocketed in Hollywood.

Left: **Actor Sir Anthony Hopkins outside Buckingham Palace after he was knighted by the Queen.**

Music

Traditional ballads, many Christmas carols, and other songs came to North America from the English and Celtic tradition. Originating in the British Isles, these songs traveled with immigrants to the New World and often adapted so well they became an entirely different kind of music. The bluegrass music of Appalachia is one such example. Now influences travel both ways. Having grown up with the American sounds of Elvis Presley, Chuck Berry, Little Richard, blues, jazz, and Motown, English rock groups of the 1960s and 70s, such as The Beatles, The Rolling Stones, Eric Clapton, and The Who later became immensely popular in the United States. English groups such as Oasis and Bush entertain audiences on both sides of the Atlantic.

Elizabethan Quebec? — Renaissance Faires

Originally set up in 1963 to educate people about Elizabethan England, Renaissance faires are a summer favorite in North America. They all feature food, drink, and entertainment as experienced in sixteenth-century England. Street theater, jugglers and, with luck, a guest appearance by the "queen" draw huge crowds every year.

Above: **The Beatles remain one of England's most successful exports. In the 1960s they took the world by storm and toured America in 1964. Here they are seen rehearsing for an appearance on the "Ed Sullivan Show."**

English Writers

With the number of recent movies based on Jane Austen's novels, it is perhaps no wonder that this nineteenth century writer is experiencing renewed popularity. The Jane Austen Society, with members all over the English-speaking world, encourages both serious study and lighthearted entertainment based on her life and work. Her novels and plays are usually quiet satires of English society and of the relations between men and women. Other English writers who have influenced modern literature include D.H. Lawrence and Thomas Hardy. Poets such as Lord Byron and Percy Bysshe Shelley, who typified the Romantic Movement of the eighteenth and nineteenth centuries, are still widely read today.

The film, *Babe*, has brought the work of the Yorkshire-based author, Dick King-Smith to the attention of North American audiences. Originally titled *The Sheep-Pig*, the story of Babe and his barnyard friends is one of many animal stories King-Smith has written. Roald Dahl, who wrote bizarre stories for adults, was also a children's author. Many of his children's books, including *Matilda*, *Charlie and the Chocolate Factory* and *The Witches*, have also been made into films.

Above: **Popular English author Roald Dahl. Many of his stories have been made into well-loved films.**

Below: **Renaissance faires are popular events and a hands-on lesson in English history.**

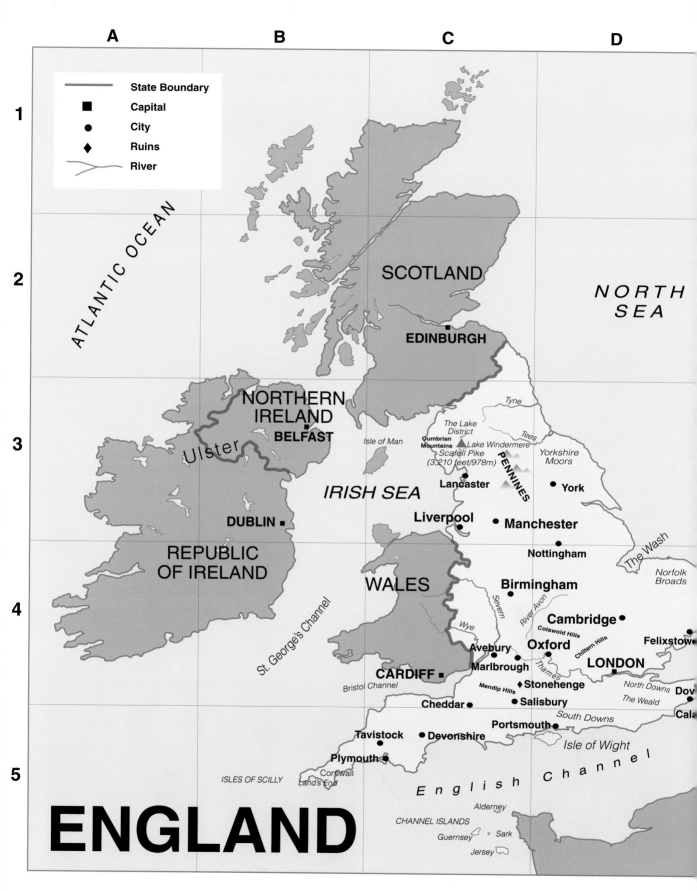

A　　**B**　　**C**　　**D**

1
2
3
4
5

State Boundary	
■	Capital
●	City
◆	Ruins
River	

ATLANTIC OCEAN

SCOTLAND

EDINBURGH

NORTH SEA

NORTHERN IRELAND

BELFAST

Ulster

Isle of Man

Tyne

The Lake District

Cumbrian Mountains

Scafell Pike (3,210 feet/978m)

Lake Windermere

Tees

Yorkshire Moors

PENNINES

IRISH SEA

Lancaster

York

DUBLIN

Liverpool

Manchester

REPUBLIC OF IRELAND

Nottingham

The Wash

Norfolk Broads

WALES

Birmingham

Severn

River Avon

Cambridge

St. George's Channel

Wye

Cotswold Hills

Chiltern Hills

Oxford

Felixstowe

Avebury

LONDON

Marlbrough

CARDIFF

Thames

Bristol Channel

Mendip Hills

◆ Stonehenge

North Downs

Dov

The Weald

Cheddar

Salisbury

South Downs

Cala

Portsmouth

Isle of Wight

Tavistock

Devonshire

English Channel

Plymouth

ISLES OF SCILLY

Cornwall

Land's End

Alderney

CHANNEL ISLANDS

Guernsey

Sark

Jersey

ENGLAND

Above: The rocky coastline of Cornwall.

Alderney C5
Atlantic Ocean A2
Avebury C4
Avon, River C4

Belfast B3
Belgium E4
Birmingham C4
Bristol Channel B4–C4

Calais E5
Cambridge D4
Cardiff C4
Channel Islands C5
Cheddar C4
Chiltern Hills D4
Cornwall B5
Cotswold Hills D4
Cumbrian Mountains C3

Devonshire C5
Dover D4
Dublin B3

Edinburgh C2
English Channel C5–D5

Felixstowe D4
France E5

Guernsey C5

Ireland, Republic of
    A4–B4
Irish Sea B3–C3
Isle of Man C3
Isle of Wight D5
Isles of Scilly B5
Jersey C5

Lake District C3
Lake Windermere C3
Lancaster C3
Land's End B5
Liverpool C3
London D4

Manchester C3
Marlbrough C4
Mendip Hills C4

Netherlands, The E4
Norfolk Broads D4
North Downs D4
North Sea D2
Northern Ireland B3
Norway E1
Nottingham D3

Oxford D4

Pennines C3
Plymouth C5
Portsmouth D5

Salisbury D4
Sark C5
Scafell Pike C3
Scotland C2
Severn River C4
South Downs D5
St. George's Channel B4
Stonehenge C5

Tavistock C5
Tees River C3
Thames D4
Tyne River C3

Ulster B3

Wales C4
Wash, The D4
Weald, The D4
Wye River C4

York D3
Yorkshire Moors D3

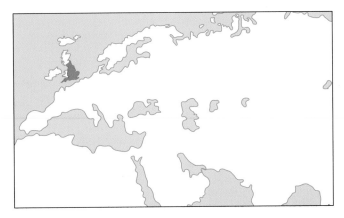

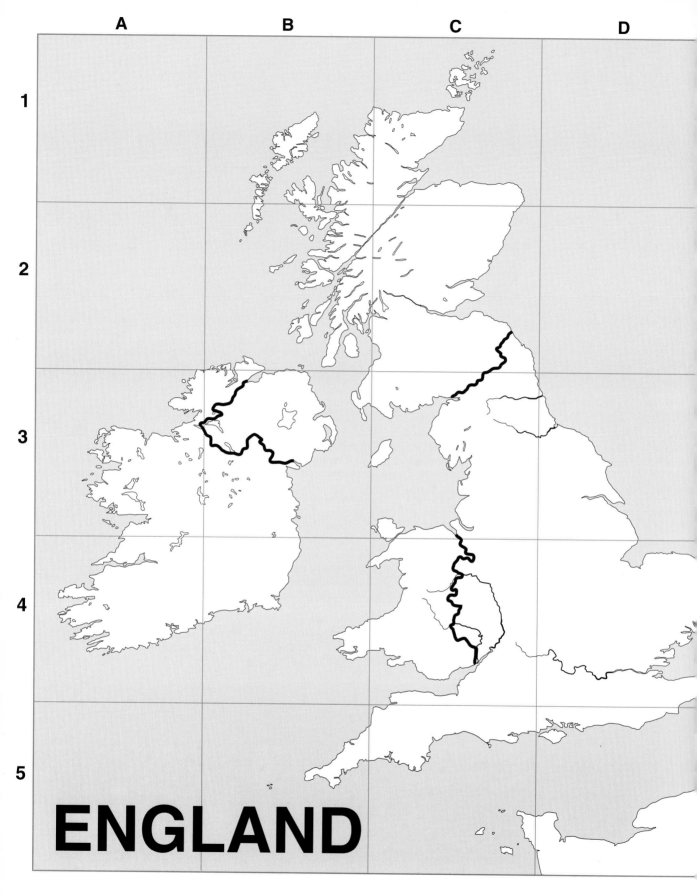

ENGLAND

How Is Your Geography?

Learning to identify the main geographical areas and points of a country can be challenging. Although it may seem difficult at first to memorize the location and spelling of major cities or the names of mountain ranges, rivers, deserts, lakes, and other prominent physical features, the end result of this effort can be very rewarding. Places you previously did not know existed will suddenly come to life when referred to in world news, whether in newspapers, television reports, or other books and reference sources. This knowledge will make you feel a bit closer to the rest of the world, with its fascinating variety of cultures and physical geography.

Used in a classroom setting, the instructor can make duplicates of this map using a copy machine (PLEASE DO NOT WRITE IN THIS BOOK!). Students can then fill in any requested information on their individual map copies. Used one-on-one, the student can also make copies of the map on a copy machine and use them as a study tool. The student can practice identifying place names and geographical features on his or her own.

England at a Glance

Official Name England (part of United Kingdom of Great Britain and Northern Ireland)

Head of State The monarch, Queen Elizabeth II (however, the country is ruled by parliament)

Head of Government The prime minister (Tony Blair as of 1997)

Area 50,000 square miles (129,500 square km)

Population 47,500,000 (England) 58,300,000 (United Kingdom)

Capital London

Major Cities Liverpool, Manchester, Birmingham, Sheffield, Leeds

Major Rivers Thames, Trent, Avon

Time Greenwich Mean Time (GMT)

Highest Point Scafell Pike 3,210 feet (978 meters)

Language English

National Anthem "God Save the Queen"

National Flag Union Flag, popularly known as the Union Jack

Religion Church of England (often called Anglican)

Main Exports Defense equipment, pharmaceuticals, oil and gas products, chemicals, food and beverages, live animals, machinery and cars, manufactured goods

Main Imports Food and beverages, live animals, manufactured goods, machinery and cars, chemicals

Currency Pound Sterling (£ 0.604 = U.S. $1 as of 1998)

Opposite: **Rescue services patrol national parks and mountain trails to ensure the safety of hikers.**

Glossary

adder: England's only native snake.

Battle of Britain: the battle between German and British air forces during World War II.

Bayeux Tapestry: a medieval embroidery, noted as both a work of art and source of history because it tells the story of the Norman Conquest.

Big Ben: the famous clock tower at the eastern end of the Houses of Parliament in London. Big Ben is famous for its accuracy and for its bell, which weighs thirteen tons. The name originally referred only to the bell but is now used for the clock itself.

British Empire: the land and countries under the ownership or control of Britain. It once included India, Australia, as well as parts of Africa and Asia.

canals: a series of waterways built to transport freight across England. Goods were transported on barges on the canals.

Celts: a group of pre-Christian people who inhabited England and other parts of Europe. They had their own language, literature, and religion presided over by the Druids, an order of priests.

chippy: English slang for a shop selling fish and chips, one of the most popular and traditional fast foods in England.

chunnel: the name given to the tunnel running under the English Channel between England and France. It allows vehicles and trains easy access between Britain and the European continent.

Commonwealth of Nations: an association of nations formerly part of the British Empire.

cricket: an English game in which two sides play against each other with bat and ball.

Crown: term referring to the monarchy, particularly in relation to its role in the government.

Crusades: a series of military expeditions between the eleventh and twelfth centuries against Muslim control of Jerusalem.

dole: a welfare benefit given to unemployed people in England.

Downing St.: the prime minister of Britain lives at 10 Downing St. in London. The term "Downing St." is often used to refer to the prime minister's office.

Elizabethan: referring to the time of the reign of Queen Elizabeth I (1558–1603).

European Union (EU): a confederation of European countries including the United Kingdom for the benefit of free trade and economic cooperation.

Great Britain: the countries of Scotland, England, and Wales combined. This does not include Northern Ireland.

hedgerows: rows of bushes or trees planted on farms as fences to control farm animals.

hobgoblins: sprites or elves present in some traditional folk tales. They are mainly depicted as house spirits responsible for tidying up or disrupting items in a house at night.

locks: an enclosed chamber in a canal for raising or lowering boats.

Magna Carta: the "Great Charter" allowing greater political and personal freedoms to the people of England. It is the foundation of parliamentary democracy.

maypole: a pole with ribbons attached to the top. During May Day celebrations people dance around the maypole while holding the ribbons. The dance is finished when the pole has been wrapped by the ribbons.

National Health Service (NHS): part of the welfare system allowing free access to health care.

National Trust: a charity that preserves places of historic interest and natural beauty.

"O" levels: high school examinations.

Old English: the language spoken in England before the development of modern English.

Oxbridge: a name referring to the Oxford and Cambridge universities. Both institutions are highly regarded for their long traditions of scholarship and high standard of education.

parliamentary democracy: the system of government developed in England allowing participation of citizens in government.

peat bogs: formed by the decay of plants in swampy ground; peat is a traditional source of fuel.

pike: a hill or mountain, as in Scafell Pike, England's highest point.

poet laureate: a poet assigned to the royal court.

prime minister: the head of the ruling party and therefore the head of the country. The ruling party is the one with a majority of seats in the House of Commons (parliament).

priory: a religious house governed by a prior or prioress, who is an officer in a religious order, below the ranking of abbot.

Reformation: the seventeenth century formation of new Protestant religions throughout Europe.

sack: to loot or plunder a place after capturing it.

soccer: a form of football – the national game of England.

standing stones: arrangements of large stone blocks thought to have been constructed during Celtic times possibly as religious monuments. Stonehenge is the most famous example.

suffragettes: early activists for women's rights. They were instrumental in gaining the right for women to vote.

"the troubles": the term used to refer to the conflict in Northern Ireland between Catholic republicans and Protestant loyalists.

United Kingdom: the combined countries of England, Scotland, Wales, and Northern Ireland.

West End: a part of London famous for its theaters.

Westminster: site of the Houses of Parliament in London and as such the seat of government.

Wimbledon: the world's most famous and prestigious tennis tournament held every year and played on grass courts.

More Books to Read

Britain. Cultures of the World series. Barbara Fuller (Marshall Cavendish)

British Food and Drink. Anna Sproule (The Bookwright Press)

England. Festivals of the World series. Harlinah Whyte (Gareth Stevens)

Francis Drake. The World's Great Explorers series. Roberta Bard (Children's Press)

Great Britain. Countries of the World series. Anna Sproule (The Bookwright Press)

Great Britain. Women in Society series. Patricia Levy (Marshall Cavendish)

Inside Great Britain. Ian James (Franklin Watts)

Kings and Queens of Britain. Frances Barnes-Murphy (Pavilion Books)

London. Cities of the World series. Conrad Stein (Children's Press)

Margaret Thatcher: First Woman Prime Minister of Great Britain. Leila Foster (Children's Press)

Passport to Great Britain. Andrew Langley (Franklin Watts)

The Tower of London. Leonard Fisher (Macmillan Publishing)

The Usborne Book of London. Moira Butterfield (Usborne Publishing)

Videos

England, Land of Splendour. (Reader's Digest Video)

Touring England. (Questar Video)

Web Sites

www.visitbritain.com/

www.cadbury.co.uk

www.ukindex.co.uk/gfawke.html

www.ukindex.co.uk/nationaltrust/info.html

Due to the dynamic nature of the Internet, some web sites may stay current longer than others. To find additional web sites, use a reliable search engine with one or more of the following keywords to help you locate information on England. Keywords: *England, English history, London, Britain, Shakespeare, Stonehenge, Wimbledon.*

Index